MAPS

John Freeman

Copper Canyon Press
Port Townsend, Washington

Cover art: Photograph by Alasdair Turner

Copper Canyon Press is in residence at Fort Worden State Park in
Port Townsend, Washington, under the auspices of Centrum. Centrum is a
gathering place for artists and creative thinkers from around the world, students
of all ages and backgrounds, and audiences seeking extraordinary cultural
enrichment.

LIBRARY OF CONGRESS CATALOGING-IN-PUBLICATION DATA

Names: Freeman, John, 1974– author.
Title: Maps / John Freeman.
Description: Port Townsend, Washington : Copper Canyon Press, 2017.
Identifiers: LCCN 2017016931 | ISBN 9781556595233 (paperback)
Subjects: LCSH: Memory — Poetry. | BISAC: POETRY / American / General.
Classification: LCC PS3606.R445465 A6 2017 | DDC 811/.6 — dc23
LC record available at https://lccn.loc.gov/2017016931

9 8 7 6 5 4 3 2 FIRST PRINTING

Copper Canyon Press
Post Office Box 271
Port Townsend, Washington 98368

www.coppercanyonpress.org

MAPS

Also by John Freeman

NONFICTION

How to Read a Novelist
The Tyranny of E-mail: The Four-Thousand-Year Journey to Your Inbox

AS EDITOR

Freeman's: The Future of New Writing
Tales of Two Americas: Stories of Inequality in a Divided Nation
Freeman's Home: The Best New Writing on Home
Freeman's Family: The Best New Writing on Family
Freeman's Arrival: The Best New Writing on Arrival
Tales of Two Cities: The Best and Worst of Times in Today's New York

For Nicole, who gave me the world

Perhaps fantasy is what you fill up maps with rather than saying that they too contain the unknown.

REBECCA SOLNIT, *A FIELD GUIDE TO GETTING LOST*

The face of God you could hardly look at. But that day it drizzled, so I could look all I wanted. I saw the homelier side. The cracked whitewash and swallows nesting in the busted end of eaves. I saw the boards sawed the size of broken windowpanes and the fruit trees, stripped. Only the tough wild rhubarb flourished. Goldenrod rubbed up their walls. It was a poor convent. I didn't see that then, but I know that now. Compared to others it was humble, ragtag, out in the middle of no place. It was the end of the world to some. Where the maps stopped.

LOUISE ERDRICH, *LOVE MEDICINE*

Contents

MAPS

ONE

Rocklin

I saw it being built in the bowl
of our foothills, trees disappearing
month after month replaced by smooth roads,
empty schools, chopped-up lots and cul-de-sacs,
unfinished houses, sound berms curving
roads into long cement smiles. We'd

drive there in our parents' cars—past
starter castles—to daisy-wheel junctions,
stoplights sheathed in muslin,
swinging slowly in summer breeze,
air so tight and piney you could hear
construction hammering miles away.

A ghost town but for that sound. We'd
sit in the unfinished high school stadium, at the
lip of what became the bleachers, a half-built
multiplex in the distance, and listen to nothing
turning into something, waiting for the sky
to go purple, traffic to hush.

Then, curfew looming, we'd race back across
the newly edgeless city, radios cranked
to drown our pounding hearts, tires whining on
the silky arterials. We felt it would never end—
the empty sky, the city that didn't matter,
holding our breath when we clicked off
the headlamps and ran through stoplights.

Beirut

For N

That rusting water tower collapsing
on its ruin was the movie theater
where lovers sat in smoky consternation
while James Bond lit his cigarettes.
The mirrored shopping mall selling
push-up jeans and gleaming watches
used to be the souk, where an old man
sold *za'atar* for small change.

Here, on the corner, where your
father explained to a gun in his mouth:
he was driving back to the
apartment to pick up the dog you left
behind, here, the apartment given
to the head of the Deuxième Bureau,
because when such a man asked for a
favor, he didn't ask, and you didn't say no.

This corner, where the sea shines in the
near distance, where Marianne was shot
through the mouth and wondered, as she
lay, if another bullet would come. Over here,
at that shop where we found the mother-of-
pearl table, the hotel where snipers played
God and the flies on the corpses in the street
rippled when the fallen were merely
wounded, and still fair game. Here,

where everywhere was somewhere else,
and the street signs point to Paris and the
invisible city calls through its sarcophagus

6

a thousand years, we move like ghosts.
The light is not to be trusted. It has been so
easily redirected. We orient through
the night, following the wind, listening for a
sudden noise, waiting for the taste of ashes.

Legend

My father's father rode the rails
west into Grass Valley and buried three children
in the shadow of a tree that spread its arms around his bakery.
Cold nights he saw stars he didn't
believe existed, and heard wild animals
howling with a loneliness he knew.

Wife dead, every morning
he woke to the bread and chill, horses
snuffling in the dark. He'd starved
before, in Canada, winter so ragged it
killed the dog, and this grief was that
feeling, shifted north into his chest.

The heart is not a diamond pressed down
into something hard like rock, but, rather, the word
my father's father said to himself
those too-cold California nights when
all he could see was the work ahead of him,
the dead behind —

her name.
He'd say her name.

The Unknowing

My grandfather was born after the earthquake and
    fire, began work at four, buried his mother at six.
Summers he picked prunes in the valley,
    sun-seared spots on his narrow shoulders.
He lost an eye. Blew out his left eardrum
    in a packing-plant accident.

He didn't make friends, a luxury
    time could not afford, smoked
through college while doubling
    as an accountant, dedicating nights to numbers,
pleasure in the orderly arrangement of the known.
    A gift, my father was born at the end of the
Great Depression to my grandfather's German wife — unaware of
    the rubble from which he emerged.

A child among the fragrant groves
    of Sacramento imported to give a desert
town some shade. Given a '57 Chevy
    at sixteen, my father rolled it twice
driving home from football games,
    license never suspended, too easy
to make such things go away. His father,
    midclimb into the airless summit of his
unexpected career, did not attend his games.

The sting of failure learned unobserved.

    Davis, then Berkeley, then seminary,
where, among closeted homosexuals
    and anguished penitents, my father felt in God
a familiar sense of bruised neglect.

He dropped out, worked as a prison
guard with teenagers put away for
    knife fights and petty thievery,
one year, peripheral vision and dropstep
    adjusted, never softened.

I was born in Cleveland, where he moved
    for more school yet sensed the developing sinkhole.
My mother, cute as a young nurse,
    from an Ohio land-grant family who paid her
credit-card bills. They lived near Woodland,
    he wore zipper boots, drove a dropped '69 Mustang.
It took years to conceive. Their gratitude for children
    was immense.
A brick thrown at his head from a passing bus
    reminded him that though he felt an outsider,
the color of his skin appeared white.

Nights in Long Island and then
    Pennsylvania, his lips on our heads,
    so kind as to be unnoticed. We slept unbroken.
I don't remember once having dinner after six.
    Our biggest complaint, the wait before we could
race out into the humid falling dark to hear
    the pop of the ball against our mitts.

Thirty years after he left Sacramento, we returned,
    his mother long since dead. The sun poured
    down on our backs at the swim club, sunspots scorched
onto our broad shoulders. Waking to mists, to tinny clock-radio top-
    forty hits, we sleepwalked to the garage
in the gloaming, where at five he stood
    counting newspapers sprung from their plastic
wrappers, my brothers and I pedaling into the fog to

the squeal and crank of our bicycles.
Halfway through the route, we'd come upon his car,
rear gate agape, Bach aerating the silence,
    a lightship docked among the palm fronds
of an indifferent neighborhood mapped by
    a developer who had long since died. He tosses
    us another forty papers, packed roughly
and quickly so that we never finished later
    than six.

Sarajevo (Summer 2016)

She pointed, two hundred meters: *there.* I was
fifteen. We were drinking wine outside
a bookshop. The shelling lasted
all night. The ruby-colored sunset, the river

close. The theater so crowded
people sat in one another's laps. Bombs fell so near every
few minutes, parts of the stage splintered.

I'm leaning on a car, cool
metal, smoked glass. The actors,
she tells me, didn't flinch, didn't miss
a single line. The audience

didn't move, didn't
make a sound.

You're here; you survived;
and you're there —
floor shaking, streets buckle —
watching a play that
for eternity will last.

Swap Meet

Stingrays black as bats,
hoods forked open flashing piston heads, Lincolns
with suicide doors,
throat-red interiors, steering wheels
spoked like spiderwebs —
we admired the catch, cowl induction
scoops spit-ragged clean, Mustangs with
cherry-red drive shafts, VWs small and tidy,
an unwrapped child's toy, then home in silence,
backs stuck to the vinyl mesh, the glow of beauty polluting
the present with an afterwash that should have cast
scale to our shabby Chevy with its
watered-down V-6 and hole in the floor.
We stopped at Orange Julius
until our backs were dry, a lesson
in possession, sweat drying
on my father's beard.

Bomb Shelters of the Oligarchs

Five hundred feet below the park
tunnels stretch for miles.
Blast-proof titanium corridors
lit by low-voltage Bruck pendants.
Mario the guardsman crawled
to freedom to escape Tiso's
Slovakia. Ten years he's
put on a blue Caraceni suit
and plunged into the earth's
inner hush, cutting a motion-
sensor'd wedge of light
into the vault's violet dark.

He's never had a visitor, unless
you count the butcher
who weekly restocks the Kobe
steaks, the sommelier who tests
the humidity of the cellar, the
mechanic who runs the 1969
Bentley, never driven, for
six minutes each day, and the
veterinarian who feeds the
Bornean elephant seven hundred
pounds of cabbage,
acacia leaves, and carrots
dropped into its cell
by a dumbwaiter secreted into
Holland Park's wading pool.

Twice an hour Mario
passes the first-edition library,
the room of jewels, the

warehouse of art, as big and cool
as St. Paul's Cathedral,
the hidden harem,
TV turned up high, reality
programs in Russian. Midday,
he kneels on the settee
by his post and unwraps a butter
sandwich and chews slowly,
drawing out the time before he
must adjust his blink rate and
return to his post, and wait for
the call, the one that never comes.

Maps

The retired consul general
lately sailed to Algiers.
He lived there in the '70s,
his wife would find body parts
in the trash some mornings,
and their baby, born white
in a hospital room choked by
flies, doctors terrified —
a child wrenched into the
world without hair, the lone
French nurse begging them
to leave: *I cannot guarantee
the safety of your child here.*

But now the child is grown,
married to an Iranian, living
in Dubai, building
wealth for a multinational bank,
while the other child — the one
the retired consul general
jokes was not a *pied-noir* —
finds in the tiny aperture
of Stockholm's daylight
ways to protect the foodstuffs
of Europe from infectious
diseases. *It is safe there now*
in Algiers, the retired consul general
says, allowing
the word's opposite to grow
in our imagination as we pick at
artichoke ravioli and swirl
the wine, an excellent wine

from Ancona, aged
in the dark for years
for us to drink in Rome
in an apartment that looks down
on the city. *It is safe,* he says again,
and the light is stupendous,
and the road that inks
the coastline nearly passable
now, and he smiles at how
he has given us benediction,
an unsolicited gift, these Roman
roads, the sunshine, this dust,
the food, the gratitude
of those used to the killing
when, finally, it stops, its
architects greeted when they
sail into port with tea and sweets,
and bread and forgetting.

Of Rockets

Molecule torn from molecule, a path
for sound. A rumbling
like thunder, with none
of its gentleness, or light.

Our near dark. Fifty
jet engines fired at full thrust,
to go nowhere.

We needed them, to do nothing
but make the air their own.

We were their own.

Reared in the silence
of an aftermath.
Their projection of power
was our home.

Everything,
the ticking quiet of the car
when it came to rest,
the blue ridge of twilight,

the vibration in church
after the organ stopped,
before we closed our books,

it all depended
on the signal that if needed

we could rain fire from the sky.

The base is closed now seven years,
wars now fought by joystick.
The silence is deadly.

We don't know violence exists
until it's recorded. Queue
the usual suspects and crowds.

Across the globe, a girl rides home
in East Sacramento
bicycle spokes shining in the twilight.

The Boy under the Car

That night in Damascus
her job was to put
tea and cake,
a sprig of mint,
on a silver tray
and walk down
the crushed-pebble drive
to the boy paid
to sleep under the car.
She never said
his name, or what
he looked like,
or whether, when she came
upon him,
curled up,
eyes black and glossy,
she caught him
singing to himself,
before the clattering metal
made him silent.

The Blinding

If we
could make
an atlas
of pain
most land
would be
terra incognita.

Summer 1995

Three rooms, sight unseen, rented from a nurse and
her husband, the floors filthy, one working burner
on the stove. Every morning I left her behind
in bed, holding me with a fierceness
I did not recognize as desperation, because
both of us were blind, we had invented this,
the parenthesis of a day between lovemaking,
meals cooked naked, novels read to each other
aloud, the slow walks to a train station, floating,
holding hands as if one of us might zeppelin
away if untethered, and the pain, a knife through
the chest, at departing for just a few days.
I had six jobs, one for a traffic-planning
firm; Tom and I would drive in the dawn hours
to an intersection, lay hose, then count cars
through our hangovers as they rolled to a four-
way stop. Someone, somewhere, would use
this data to widen roads, erect new signs,
trim the summit ash and red oak so that drivers
could reduce their speed in time. Astonishing
to realize there was such a thing as too much
beauty. I was nineteen, I had another lifetime to
learn this; all I could do then was stand
near the flame, and marvel at the blisters.

Barbers

From the hotel in Martyr's Square
drive east into Achrafieh in
search of a barber learn
there are four words for barber
three of which are spit out
the last of which — *coiffeur* — anoints
a tongue with its mellifluence
like the milky coffee served by
the small woman from Khartoum who
never stops bending and refilling
to sit with a group of men wearing
three-piece suits fingering
prayer beads and crosses
to watch a man larger than most
giggle his way through a
haircut he has some advice
for what one ought
to do with sideburns too long
and my beard it is not good
there are ways to fix this and
these men who in another
time would have had other advice
and other things to offer
gather around to officiate as
the coiffeur takes a blade to
the neck and trims until
my head is as smooth and
perfumed as a past
not past but present.

Coins

The crowd rotates by chemical signals
fired into synaptic gaps,
zeros and ones shot into space,
downloaded onto screens, reassembled
into words instructing Parisians to gather
at République by six, that they do in
the thousands, and begin their waltz
around the draped statue that shows
how good ideas must be held aloft,
abstracted, like twelve lives turned
to martyrs' treasure, one side
of a coin depicting decadence
and insult, the other, tendered here,
brave insouciance before backward
ideals. A cannon puff announces
their transcendence, from
lives into paper lanterns, rising
from the hands of figures in
black who've mounted the plinth like security agents of justice.
Glowing white orbs drift
upward through the silvery
drizzle and thousands
cheer as one, unified,
tonight, as somewhere else
thousands are too in
agreement that a life is not
just a life, but a vessel
for the value we assign it.

You Are Here

When I arrive subway tokens coin
a pocket like teeth, XXX parlors
gum 6th Avenue south of 34th.
We park at Astor on Wednesdays,
wait for the *Voice,* quarter roll and tennis
shoes, ready to out-sprint all comers to pay
phones, on to mythical three-bedroom apartments
under two thousand dollars.

Everybody takes the subway, the 6, the J,
the N, hips glued to one another.
The F train stop at 2nd Avenue hot as a
smokehouse, we stand over grates
for a whisper of air, land at
Allen Street, three rooms rump-side
of a tenement that rattles when semis
run the Houston light after dark. One day
there'll be a train carving south straight
through those greasy foundations.

Be patient, they've been planning it
since 1929. The city grinds
its molars at night, carefully mined
explosions boring cavities beneath
Manhattan, while other lines
ride all hours in yellow light, gliding
to stops at the zebra-painted beam
halfway down each platform,
conductor always pointing up, as if
to say, yes, you are here.

The Heat

At night its
warble strummed to
silence
the crabgrass
blue, then green,
then black,
the branches relax and
gently scratch the screen like
a dark-haired woman
who years later would
pluck it so that she
could be let in.

TWO

Still Life

From after dark

until early morning,

at the kitchen

table, writing

patient notes,

the radio turned low:

Leonard with HIV,

whose steroids didn't

work; the dying mother

of a famous rock star,

alone in her Vacaville villa

bemedaled in memorabilia,

the son's biggest fan.

Her own disease

lying in wait.

Then, as we slept,

it crept to her shoulder,

capped her pen, locked

her files, and

clicked off the music.

Mail

We wrote one another a lot
those days, long winding
letters that crossed a country, in which
I asked if she knew my gratitude;
her replies so generous
it's only now I realize
my gratitude wasn't gratitude
but another request.

On Generosity

She gave so easily
we didn't know acceptance
was training us
to give back
when you opened a door
she went through first, because
the tide goes both ways.

Rehearsal

The hardwood is dusty, whorled from last night's dance,
fifteen of us lie starfished around the gym, legs bent

this way, then again, beneath dome lights caged
in their own protection, turned on half an hour ago,

flickering and blinking as if a drill, while below,
I'm having a thought about a thought,

that years from this moment I'll remember it:
lights, ceiling, handprints on the backboard —

of all topographies, this is one I hoard.

Allowances

I gave myself excuses.

This is for my pain —

and this, and this.

Terrible things.

Pain. My pain.

All of it

so I could

get on a train

twice a month

to witness yours.

The Money

The money, he asks, haven't you
thought about the money?

We're feeding her
apple sauce and yogurt.

Days later, alone on the East River
I say aloud to myself:

I don't have a fucking wallet in my heart
to put the fucking money in.

The Last

Stars beat back your kindness,
night blot the sun;
for days we counted her breaths —
and then there was only one.

Tattoo

Driving around
L.A., top down,
my brother
and I discussing how
to remember when
this yellow light
tells you to forget
and to turn around
to do something
else, just stop
being you and
become another.
We decide
on a tattoo. At
first it's not big,
it'd be discreet,
the kind you notice
like the glint of
a watch.
But, of course, as
we talk it
gets bigger, it
elaborates.
It crawls up
arms, down
our thighs, like it
needs to keep
moving, grow-
ing to outpace
what it replaces.
I say the neck is
off-limits. Finally

we have to admit
there's only
one way this
will end. What if
I get a tattoo
of her face
on my face,
is that
enough? We drive
in silence
for a mile, before
I realize that
is exactly
what a face is.

Via

In Paris
of men in red
trousers,
women with dogs.
I follow you
through their maze.

It was cool for July,
the lavender
blossoms, dusty
slap of the streets,
motorcycles, and
cigarette smoke.

Then there was
the Seine,
ancient, night with
the dignity of an un-
attended funeral.

One limestone pebble
at a time given and
never received,
the river knows everything
is taken in the end.

I lost you at the bridge,
behind Pont Marie,
twilight's night trick,
that moment a
river is a road, a path,
eternal brightness.

Repeat

I tell it so many times
    on 10th Street, over lunch
in a bar, to tender eyes,
it begins to sound
    like a piece of news —

but once I decide
    I'll tell it how
it happened —
how she starved to death,
    mumbled her pain,
clung, shat, moaned,
how I was too frightened
    to sit with her
through the night
so she wouldn't die alone.

Blackout

I'd been to the building
in '96, the upper floors un-
finished, balconies perched on
air, a new gouge at the sky below
Houston, the only rooftop with-
out a water tower. Brick by brick
it claimed the neighborhood from
mean streets, its lobby swirled
with mirrors and gold, its pools
of senseless water, Albanian
doormen with tattooed wrists
who came to this city with
sacks of their dead mothers' jewels
and lethal skills to make it safe for
us. We moved in four years later,
arriving to a white box without
furniture.

Year by year, as the cafés closed
and reopened, and bodegas
shut and stayed shut, it became
a home. Here is where I learned
to paint a wall. Here is where
I discovered garlic, and poetry again,
where she held my hand when
I got the worst news, and where
we began our night walks and
had dinner and I proposed and
she said yes and we went away,
and where we returned, and it
was home, because a home is
where you return to.

And month by month as we fell out
of love, a tomb we returned to at night,
the lid drawn shut, the night
heaved, and the lives we
both lived on pause.
How much we loved each other!
We couldn't turn over in the dark to see
we were decreating something greater
the longer we waited. The lights
outside showed her face in sleep,

I should have known. Her leg gave out first.
A stress fracture from too much running.
Her body returned to how it was the day we met,
broken but beautiful. And all that final night,
sprawled in the heat of the city's
blackout, her crutches leaned against
the wall like rifles, she seethed with
what I hadn't done. Until I proposed
the obvious. I put her on my back and
carried her down the stairs, eleven
flights to Houston. The firelights
blinking on the generator
heat. The cement stairs chipped and gray.
The pause at each landing. The growing
noise from the neighborhood kids,
for whom this was a great night, a joyous
night, the feeling of her weight
on my back, knowing she hated me,
knowing that when we got to the bottom,
and pushed out the air lock of those
silly pools and swirls of gold, out into
the heavy night, and she could crutch on
her own across the street, she wouldn't
look back. And she didn't.

Tautology

She sends me a
photograph from
a small Denver
cemetery, shot
by camera phone.
I wonder if that's her long
shadow behind
the headstone
bearing our names;
I wonder, too,
if the crunched
leaves scattered there
made her briefly
nostalgic, or
thoughtful, before
she snapped and
swiped the forward
button, remarking
Look, John,
we're dead.

Oslo

I've been here
before, hotels
in bluish light,
squares of ice.
Outside the city
opera house
taxi tires
crunch on pavements
of salt, first
departures. I begin
a letter describing the day,
knowing you'll
never read it. Later,
among the commuters,
I'm on the street,
and, for an instant,
I feel
you're here.
Ice, lights,
the wind's knowing sere.
It's been two years.

Ides

And so
begins the rain,
stereo needle
lowered to
waiting disc,
volume raised
until a song
is heard.

Saudade

means nostalgia, I'm told, but also
nostalgia for what never was. Isn't it
the same thing? At a café
in Rio flies wreathe my glass.

How you would have loved this: the waiter
sweating his knit shirt dark. Children
loping, in tiny suits or long shorts, dragging
toys and towels to the beach. We talk,

or I talk, and imagine your answer, the heat clouding our view.
Here, again, grief fashioned in its cruelest translation:
my imagined you is all I have left of you.

THREE

English Hours, Three Pieces of Advice

For Peter Carey

Join a gym; find a pub;
don't forget to
walk, this last
part the easiest
to follow
especially after
you told
of the old
horse-track oval
leaving a
spectral halo
around Stanley
Gardens.
Home late, I
find myself
circling the cream-
white houses,
limestone crescents,
the somber churches
and dimmed bistros,
going back, further
back, until I don't
know whether
I'm arriving.
You, for whom two
places are
one place,
understand this
sense of vertigo
sometimes means
you're home.

Night Bus to Richmond

Suddenly it's upon me,
scything the night
like a red knife,
three passengers,
specimens in vinegar glow.
On the upper deck
a woman is reading *Catch-22,*
the dream having erased
the cold rubber floor mats,
the diesel rattle,
a gray December night
a man walks up a hill
toward home.

On Love

If wind asked permission
we might wait and listen
as if night stopped its blue
curtain and wheat bent without scattering
its hope of what happens in the dark,
and happens by accident.

Wimbledon

Walking on the common
    in heavy blue light,

she says to him the time for children,
    were there ever one, has

passed, that would be that, and
    two close calls aside,

she proves to be right, and the years
    pass with happiness

too great to be measured, because
    one does not measure what feels

endless, just as this land was once
    a queen's private hunting estate,

everything around it Hers too;
    there were no boundaries,

until a village grew to service
    Her horses and

part-time tailors, the cobblers and
    surgeons and cooks needed

to properly entertain guests, and
    then the uninvited came,

took what was not desirable, built
    their limestone houses,

rolled carriages down two-track
    paths until the dirt was stone,

watching the eternal from their
    handblown windows

as it tilted through centuries, like
    a faithful planet

that doesn't regard its reflection
    bouncing off distant moons,

light traveling back so slowly the
    world has moved on, its orbit

endless, drawn by forces
    exerting their will in the darkness,

which on this falling January night
    has drawn the sky close

like a wool coat, the lights in
    homes once run by servants

flickering without a wince of post-
    imperial shame,

and South London looks up
    at wisdom winging down

at them like a bat flying on sonar:
    how nothing remains, that in

mere years, their love, with no one
    but each other as witness,

will have found some other way
    to mark time, not by being

boundless, but bound, as the sky
    is to ground at the close of day.

Lacking Measures

I have been here forty days and most nights — as
the air thins

to evening chills and the cold white lozenge of
the moon licks

the sky white round its edges, I try to
understand

why I have put myself in a place where all I can
do is watch myself

think. And then think about that thought.

I imagine if I open my skull like a gourd there
would merely be

another head inside, an overgrown seed,
and inside that one

yes another one, and so on. At least they are
mine, but I wonder

what bitter ground they grow from. I am not
however to ask myself

this question, it is macro-temporal,
impossible to know

and, they say, incapable of being changed.

3

We treat the brain so that we can deal with
the mind, my indulgent

doctor tells me, as if I have sprained my ankle,
his legs crossed

showing bone-white shank wrapped in argyle,
a sinister Christmas

stocking. After each conversation I am allowed
to smoke and after

each smoke I return to the room and cry over
what I have done

and swear to my dead mother it is not her fault
and then the night returns

with its black scarf.

4

If I am lucky I have the moon's mute worry to
imagine and pray to,

which is the same thing, and what frightens
me more than

her silence, or the tick and creak of such a large
building in the hours

when there are just three digits on the clock,

is how similar being here is to being dead. My life
has been abandoned

like a ship set ablaze and left to drift at sea,
where there is the time

you can see it float away, and then when it
is spied in the distance,

lost at latitude, then it falls from the
map altogether, and it's as if it

were never there at all.

Maddy

Then a swift left turn. Her nose
tilts to the breeze feathering
her hair, eyes closed in pleasure
or curiosity or rapture, I don't know,
so much of what she does
remains a mystery, as I'm
sure we remain for her,
and she stands there pointing to
a new day, as she has four
thousand times before,
no diminishment or boredom,
as if this were the first breeze
she ever smelled, filled with
magic and dog weed and
bus fuel and fox crap, and
burglars, last night's
laundry entering the
spin cycle, and she
stands there, poised in
arthritic grandeur, seven years
into her overbred, illness-plagued,
brief life, showing us
hope is routine, is hope.

28th Street

All the years we lived behind
the florists, when I used to wake early
to stand by the window and watch
the men in red sweatshirts pushing
dollies of hydrangeas, tulips on pallets
from Holland, pale pink
ranunculus, crowds of yellow
hyacinths, a fury of color beneath
halogen lamps all before the hour
of six. The restaurant owners in
black leather jackets who came
before dawn were made to stand like
courtiers before this beauty, to
await its assembly while across
the street someone was usually pissing
with leisure in the car park.

Childhood in Emmaus

Every night the walls

vibrated to the evening's drag strip,

light-to-light races skimming the hills, and

big-block octaves poured down our

brain stems as the sun set. It was a small

Pennsylvania town full of cars on blocks,

jacked-up Novas and tricked-out Chevelles, asphalt lawns,

and redbrick ranches. A decent man

didn't have clean hands. There had been

a mill once, and what innocence

remained sang its song, night by night.

It was our rock art, semitone lullaby,

slapback echo of V-8s against the hills,

a supercharged tinnitus, four-barrel whomp, cars —

revved-up cars for men with no release.

Witness This

Every April we unsheathed sofa cushions from their wrappers, perched tea on our laps, and became an audience for his four-decade victory lap — the Great Wall, the Blue Lagoon, the Panama Canal, the unsmiling projection of him and his second wife against the world's great achievements, as if his dodging the sinkhole were an epic that needed witnesses besides his own camera.

Each narrated photo lingered, without joy but studied observation, dust swirling in the projector's haze, as my father sat, middle-aged, his own family seated in halo, swallowing his rage and his grief. It should have been his mother there, dressed in linen, leaning against the cool crutch of a terrace railing, the half-drunk glass of rosé ghosting a day's pleasure spent peering into Capri's too-green-to-believe water.

She was the worker, though, the one who plated dinners at five, and wiped his tears and kept him company and mixed the drinks, and told him secrets, and huddled him against her sisters' menthol'd embraces in their tiny apartments above the capitol, where they lived alone, except for when certain men came to visit and they put on furs and stepped in and out of Buicks with the practiced steps of women who knew how easily gladness combusts.

His mother's heart burst while he was away, and so there was a life, forsworn of travel, a decadence and abandonment of what mattered. So we carved our way down interstates, crammed into a car with holes in the undercarriage, inscribing our childhoods onto the Central Valley, its mean brown flats, the irrigation canals, hidden estuaries, the fields his father once worked a long time ago, before he grabbed a rung and held on with the clench of a man who knew how to survive.

My grandfather traveled into his middle nineties — leaf-season in New Hampshire, the Alaskan coast in April, the Rocky Mountain express across Canada — but he never visited his dying daughter-in-law, the one who also dreamed of Paris, and ordered cakes from England, and who read of Russian revolutions, but who saw none of it, even when he knew she was dying, and then it was too late: the sons arrowing back, the taking of turns sleeping on the sofas, the theater of morphine, the curtains' plea for privacy.

Fifty years later the post brings my father's first Christmas card since remarrying, a photograph snapped from the summit of Machu Picchu, him and his second wife, the one who travels, peering into the mist of this stony place, and I wonder what it is I am supposed to witness, other than a happiness. I wonder who this picture is for. Only my heart refuses what the eye cannot deny. And I wonder if its clench is the one that will help me survive, or the one that will keep this carousel turning.

Benchmark

Two years since
she came to me
in a dream, my sleep
these days shallow
and absent, like
dual carriageways
you see on beaches
in the off-season when
no one is there
except a man who walks
his dog as a reminder
to do something
in retirement.

Return

I went back to the city we visited, to
the restaurant, to the bar
where we saw the twilight fade
and stood outside the hotel
we returned to in the noisy night, the sleepless
doorman reading *Red Harvest,*

he wasn't there, and after hours
the city convulsed with an ugliness,
helicopters overhead to keep the crowds
of tourists at bay, and, at the bar,
the crowd wasn't so nice,
and in the restaurant I tried to find in that evening's diners some flash

of her hair or our hands across the table,
instead I caught only my reflection in the hazy mirror,
blurred and only apparently mine
when he bent as I did to finish
the meal that tasted of nothing,
not even the memory of what it was once.

Pumpkins at Night

Caged in display,
torn from roots
before ripe,
gourds full of seeds
unsown. The lights
on, beckoning
people off the slick
night street
with neon signs,
promising festivity,
but this is New York:
no one's buying it.

Fish

For Aleksandar Hemon

Americans are peculiar about breakfast,
you say as we belly to the sushi bar
in the rain, eight in the morning, man with blistered
forearms, gut-slick knife, curious where
we're from. I say New York, you say Chicago,
although I know that's a complicated
answer, yet how you've learned
to love it, as fierce as your jaws,
squared-down on cuttlefish and tuna,
eel and giant prawns, moments ago
scrabbling with twelve terrified legs
to escape their tank atop five of
their brethren; it's just breakfast,
washed down with green tea grown in
Shizuoka steeped in water from
the Arakawa River watershed.
When you first went back to Sarajevo
after the siege stranded you in America,
the water tasted different, like
ash, you say, and the cinemas
had moved, blocks of houses
plain evaporated, and most
of your friends upstream
in Montreal or Paris,
where, once, we bellied up to a
mosque tagine joint and ate
couscous with Bosnians who
chewed French words into chunks
the Moroccan chefs could understand.
You grunt, we pay, we walk in the rain

to the marketplace, dodging pushcarts
piled with ice-packed Styrofoam boxes,
cod and salmon and fish roe and smelt.
You had to see where the fish were unloaded,
so we step into that abattoir,
slip through the aisles on wooden
racks dark with blood,
peering at all the creatures
of the deep hauled up and transported
to a purgatory of ice — octopus,
and puffer fish, squid curled like
pink knuckles, tuna so big it had to
be carved by vertical saw,
the technician squinting through a
cigarette, giving us thumbs-up
after it fell in two,
a split log. Near the exit
a man holds a fugu by its neck, its tail
twitching furiously, but he
doesn't smash it, stroking its flank gently,
smoothing its perfect skin,
its scales, its green-fine body,
then his blade drawn so fast
across the neck
departure becomes a kindness.

Waiting

Days when mind swallows its periscope, I am
all skin, sinew, a walking animal. The light
on St. John's Square wakes azure blue, a sky-
bound lake. Clouds membrane the sea
like nets. Beneath it a blind, searching crustacean,
caught in its spell, I move carefully, touching
nothing, waiting for a sign to come.

Paris (Bastille Day)

Everybody is watching the doors to paradise, honey pouring bleach into words: this is not a truck, it is a weapon, curvetting, arroyoing. A flood diverting a river finds a dark vacancy in the faces of our morning. This is not a hospital, it is a target. Seven thousand killed on land mines alone. Light can be both a particle and a wave. I feel the boundaries of these stories, like basalt in hand. They leave a trace. The rock submerged in the pond bends water around it, like the relentless, inarticulate underache of anguish that culminates in violence. How we rage to create, to name, to remap the world. It is what the living do, even as the sun we see is less than half the diameter of a dime held at arm's length. We must turn from glory lest it blind us. Ermine, ocotillo, paloverde, mesquite, sand verbena, camellia, brittlebush, chokecherry, helleborine orchids. Once we poured honey into the names. They were ignored by the cutthroat trout, nesting plovers,

the water ouzel, black tadpoles, squawfish, razorbacks, wolverines, red-breasted mergansers, long-necked pintails, wigeons, and burbot. We live in the dusk lands of language. This is not a guest, this is an alien. This is not a this is

This. Remember the better names of the world. Hear the long, high whistle that sings through the gap between what is and what we call it. Let us not mistake that song for anything but a warning.

Repair

They've torn down walls, ripped up floorboards, pulled out the electrics and
    beneath all that Carolina pine discovered
blackened supporting beams so brittle I can pick off chips with my
    fingernail, as if someone had roasted marshmallows
at an open fire on the bathroom floor, and it's scorched above the tin
    ceiling tiles too, so badly the carpenter looks
at me like I've been running a dogfighting ring out of my apartment, and in
    his wince
    I know this is going to cost, like, there-goes-the-rest-of-it
cost, just as, later that summer, in the dentist's chair tipped toward the TV
    where Darlene Rodriguez is talking about
the latest MTA accident, a bus this time, which ran out of control and
    smashed into a building, killing three, including the driver.
Something similar happened on 14th Street, my dentist says, peering into
    the hole
    he's made on my back molar, the one supposed to be
a cavity but is now a root canal and a crown, and I keep apologizing to him
    and his friendly assistant, with the star tattooed
behind her ear, for the embarrassment — six years it's been,
    my job, the commuting, but I know
why I didn't go in during that time, I'm thinking
    of my father cleaning her teeth, more and more yellow
even though after she'd eat he'd raise her out of her chair and carry
    her like the fullback he once was, lifting her off the ground into
    the bathroom,
slowly brushing her teeth, wiping the spit, drool,
    the toothpaste with a washcloth, and when I visited
I'd stand there helpless before so much love, unable to do anything
    useful except
    to watch how serious it gets, how there's nothing serious
without an end, and that's the only bill you're ever going to be scared to pay,
    unthinkable, because once you start paying, there's no end

to what you'll give, and I witnessed him do it, no bargaining, no
        installment, just
    give up everything, his vanity first, then his friendships,
and finally his faith. He looked at the blackened circle around her and asked
    if this is how God takes then we don't have an agreement
anymore, while I'm recording the changes
    in him, so great they just obliterate any
self-consciousness, it becomes something you do, like carpentry or dentistry,
    if you don't drill this tooth now you're going to lose it,
if you don't give these drivers a break they're going to fall asleep at the wheel
    and smash into things. So I take the rest of the money
I earned from her death, this wealth drilled from the ground in Texas and
    Indiana and Oklahoma, Rockefeller money that
bought my grandmother a sterling retirement and would have passed to
        my mother
    if she hadn't died before her own, I take the money and put
it back into the new hole, and the carpenter doesn't blink,
    or even say thank you, just says he'll make it look
like new, both he and I know he's lying.

In the Heart of the Night

1

I wake in the dark from a dream,
driving to Utica again,
it's snowing and we're late.
I carry the Knausgaard
down to the hotel lobby for a
beer in the mortuary silence
of sleep's gravity. The restaurant's
closed, the waiters and waitresses
drinking behind shutters,
laughing and joking in Poiish. Young
Knausgaard is watching himself at age seven,
heart on display, already skeptical
of his own surveillance: "It should be
allowed to beat in secret,
hidden from our sight…
you understood that when you saw it,
a little animal without eyes";
but of course
the heart has eyes,
not its own,
and we watch ourselves
watching it, as much our heart
as the heart itself.

2

How easily I
recall those first days.
I paced your bookshelves, you kept
pouring coffee, the hours into
single digits,
your beauty,

how I watched my heart
know your beauty would
possess me
the rest of my life.

    3

And that other night,
when I was alone with her,
reading, to keep from
hearing her breathe, it
was the last night, I was
last to sit with her, I could
not bear to think she might
die alone, the silence, how
it pressed down, and her
breathing, it came in waves
and would stop for seconds
at a time, then again,
this erratic shore; and the
waiting had exhausted me,
overcame my desire
to be the one good son
so you came down to do
what I could not do, which
was to sit through that half silence
until morning, while I slept
at your feet in relief.

    4

A gentle silence, this night
I can't be with you,
the rattle of the streets
pushes me outside,
the row of shops
across from the hotel —

an off-license, closed, a
Thai bar, people stand outside
smoking, and a hair salon, in which
I see two figures entwined
on a couch in the dark.
It's late, and
I can't imagine why
they'd still be there.
A bus passes
and the shop is there again
and they're up,
moving around in the dark,
it doesn't seem possible, but
it looks to me like
they're dancing.

Acknowledgments

The following poems appeared in slightly different form at: "The Boy under the Car" (*Boston Review*); "Blackout," "Fish" (*Brick*); "The Heat," "Oslo," "The Unknowing" (*Buenos Aires Review*); "English Hours, Three Pieces of Advice," "Legend," "Repeat" (*The Common*); "Bomb Shelters of the Oligarchs" (*Harvard Review*); "Maps," "28th Street" (*H.O.W. Journal*); "Coins," "Paris (Bastille Day)," "Repair," "Wimbledon" (*The Iowa Review*); "The Blinding," "Summer 1995" (*Narrative*); "Barbers" (*The Nation*); "Allowances," "Rocklin" (*The New Yorker*); "Beirut," "The Money" (*The Paris Review*); "The Last," "Mail" (*Prairie Schooner*); "Return," "Witness This" (*Virginia Quarterly Review*); "Still Life," "Tattoo" (*Zyzzyva*).

About the Author

John Freeman is the editor of *Freeman's*, a literary biannual, and author of two books of nonfiction, *The Tyranny of E-mail* and *How to Read a Novelist*. He has also edited two anthologies of writing on inequality, *Tales of Two Cities* and *Tales of Two Americas*. The former editor of *Granta*, he lives in New York, where he teaches at The New School and is writer-in-residence at New York University. The executive editor at *LitHub*, he has published poems in *Zyzzyva*, *The New Yorker*, *The Paris Review*, and *The Nation*. His work has been translated into more than twenty languages.

Lannan Literary Selections

For two decades Lannan Foundation has supported the publication and distribution of exceptional literary works. Copper Canyon Press gratefully acknowledges their support.

LANNAN LITERARY SELECTIONS 2017

John Freeman, *Maps*

Rachel McKibbens, *blud*

W.S. Merwin, *The Lice*

Javier Zamora, *Unaccompanied*

Ghassan Zaqtan (translated by Fady Joudah), *The Silence That Remains*

RECENT LANNAN LITERARY SELECTIONS FROM COPPER CANYON PRESS

Josh Bell, *Alamo Theory*

Mark Bibbins, *They Don't Kill You Because They're Hungry, They Kill You Because They're Full*

Malachi Black, *Storm Toward Morning*

Marianne Boruch, *Cadaver, Speak*

Jericho Brown, *The New Testament*

Olena Kalytiak Davis, *The Poem She Didn't Write and Other Poems*

Michael Dickman, *Green Migraine*

Deborah Landau, *The Uses of the Body*

Sarah Lindsay, *Debt to the Bone-Eating Snotflower*

Maurice Manning, *One Man's Dark*

Camille Rankine, *Incorrect Merciful Impulses*

Roger Reeves, *King Me*

Paisley Rekdal, *Imaginary Vessels*

Brenda Shaughnessy, *So Much Synth*

Richard Siken, *War of the Foxes*

Frank Stanford, *What About This: Collected Poems of Frank Stanford*

Ocean Vuong, *Night Sky with Exit Wounds*

Poetry is vital to language and living. Since 1972, Copper Canyon Press has published extraordinary poetry from around the world to engage the imaginations and intellects of readers, writers, booksellers, librarians, teachers, students, and donors.

WE ARE GRATEFUL FOR THE MAJOR SUPPORT PROVIDED BY:

THE PAUL G. ALLEN
FAMILY FOUNDATION

Anonymous

Jill Baker and Jeffrey Bishop

Donna and Matt Bellew

John Branch

Diana Broze

Sarah and Tim Cavanaugh

Janet and Les Cox

Mimi Gardner Gates

Linda Gerrard and Walter Parsons

Gull Industries, Inc.
on behalf of Ruth and William True

The Trust of Warren A. Gummow

Steven Myron Holl

Phil Kovacevich and Eric Wechsler

Lakeside Industries, Inc.
on behalf of Jeanne Marie Lee

TO LEARN MORE ABOUT UNDERWRITING
COPPER CANYON PRESS TITLES,
PLEASE CALL 360-385-4925 EXT. 103

WE ARE GRATEFUL FOR THE MAJOR SUPPORT PROVIDED BY:

Maureen Lee and Mark Busto
Rhoady Lee and Alan Gartenhaus
Ellie Mathews and Carl Youngmann as The North Press
Anne O'Donnell and John Phillips
Petunia Charitable Fund and advisor Elizabeth Hebert
Suzie Rapp and Mark Hamilton
Joseph C. Roberts
Jill and Bill Ruckelshaus
Cynthia Lovelace Sears and Frank Buxton
Kim and Jeff Seely
Catherine Eaton Skinner and David Skinner
Dan Waggoner
Austin Walters
Barbara and Charles Wright
The dedicated interns and faithful volunteers
of Copper Canyon Press

The Chinese character for poetry is made up of two parts: "word" and "temple." It also serves as pressmark for Copper Canyon Press.

This book is set in Minion, with headings set in Arno, both designed for digital composition by Robert Slimbach. Book design by VJB/Scribe. Printed on archival-quality paper.